THE PLENARY POWER

OF THE HON'BLE SUPREME COURT OF INDIA
UNDER ARTICLE 142 OF THE CONSTITUTION

RADHA SHYAM JENA

BLUEROSE PUBLISHERS
India | U.K.

Copyright © Radha Shyam Jena 2025

All rights reserved by author. No part of this publication may be reproduced, stored in a retrieval system or transmitted in any form or by any means, electronic, mechanical, photocopying, recording or otherwise, without the prior permission of the author. Although every precaution has been taken to verify the accuracy of the information contained herein, the publisher assume no responsibility for any errors or omissions. No liability is assumed for damages that may result from the use of information contained within.

BlueRose Publishers takes no responsibility for any damages, losses, or liabilities that may arise from the use or misuse of the information, products, or services provided in this publication.

For permissions requests or inquiries regarding this publication, please contact:

BLUEROSE PUBLISHERS
www.BlueRoseONE.com
info@bluerosepublishers.com
+91 8882 898 898
+4407342408967

ISBN: 978-93-6783-962-1

Cover design: Daksh
Typesetting: Tanya Raj Upadhyay

First Edition: April 2025

DEDICATION

I owe my Reverend Parents

LATE SHRI BHAGBAN JENA

AND

LATE SMT. GIRIJA DEVI

for inspiring me to study law despite their grinding poverty. Their inspiration still lives through me as I have dedicated myself with pure devotion to this legal profession for the destitute and aggrieved. Their moral support is impalpable and helps me encounter uphill with valour and dynamism.

ABOUT THE AUTHOR

[The contents of the back (cover) page be replaced with this content]

Radha Shyam Jena (R.S. Jena) is a sincere practicing lawyer and an Advocate-on-Record in the Hon'ble Supreme Court of India since 1995. Many cases argued by him have been reported and are available in the SCC and Judgment Today. He has also written many articles on legal and other subjects to bring his ideas and thoughts to the knowledge of the common people in general, published in the English daily esteemed newspaper "Kalinga Chronicle" from Bhubaneswar, Odisha. This book is his maiden publication. The author expects encouragement and inspiration for further writing. Any suggestion may please be made by the readers for the improvement of the standard of his writing.

The author is ready to accept any fair criticism from the bottom of his heart.

Mr. Radha Shyam Jena

PREFACE

This book contains the important judgments of the Hon'ble Supreme Court of India empowered to exercise its plenary power under Article 142 of the Constitution. For the sake of dispensation of complete justice, the Hon'ble Supreme Court can use the power under Article 142 of the Constitution as a complementary where no statute has to help the parties/litigants to a case before the Hon'ble Supreme Court. The framers of the Constitution have endowed the Hon'ble Supreme Court of India with the plenary power to provide justice to a genuine party to a dispute. The judgments based on Article 142 of the Constitution would undoubtedly enlighten the students of the law as to under what circumstances the Hon'ble Supreme Court can exercise its power under Article 142. The judgments referred herein on Article 142 have been narrated in compendium for the sake of reference.

This book would help the law students, the budding lawyers grasp the various important judgments to enlighten them in no time the unimpeachable and pragmatic power of the Apex Court vested with after a long deliberation of the constituent assembly. The Article 142 bears a substantial force to obviate a constitutional crisis. The author is, therefore, seeks better suggestions to enlighten himself for the betterment of the lawyers economically sound or not. Still, they will inspire citizens and encourage them to pin faith in the Constitution. The judgments referred in the book are prodigious and insightful and therefore it would undoubtedly create anxiety and enthusiasm to study the Constitution and its contribution to create a serene milieu in the highly populous country like India.

A sincere and diligent endeavour has been made, the best possible to avoid errors and omissions. Suggestions are invited from the readers at heart to help improve the next edition. Being sole author of the book, I express my gratitude to my steno namely Bhanubhuvan Upadhyay for dictation and type-setting of the script of the book with all sincerity as well as Bluerose Publishers for the publication of the book.

LIST OF CASES REFERRED

1. Prem Chand Garg Vs. Excise Commissioner, U.P., Allahabad (1963) Supp. (1) SCR 885
2. State of Rajasthan & Ors. Etc. Etc. Vs. Union of India Etc. Etc. (1977) 3 SCC 592
3. State of Karnataka Versus Union of India & Anr., (1977) 4 SCC 608
4. A.R. Antulay Vs R.S. Nayak & Anr., (1988) 2 SCC 602
5. Vinay Chandra Mishra (1995) 2 SCC 584
6. Consumer Education and Research Centre Versus Union of India & Ors., (1995) 3 SCC 42 at para 28
7. Pt. Shamboo Nath Tikoo & Ors. Versus S. Gian Singh & Ors., (1995) Supp. 3 SCC 266
8. Bonkya Alias Bharatshivaji Mane & Ors. Vs State of Maharashtra (1995) 6 SCC 447
9. Delhi Development Authority Versus Skipper Construction Company (P) Ltd. & Anr., (1996) 4 SCC 622
10. C. Chenga Reddy and Others Versus State of A.P. (1996) 10 SCC 193
11. Supreme Court Bar Association Versus Union of India & Anr., (1998) 4 SCC 409
12. M/s Essar Constructions Versus M.P. Ramakrishna Reddy (2000) 6 SCC 94

13. M.C. Mehta Versus Kamal Nath & Ors., (2000) 6 SCC 213
14. State of Andhra Pradesh Vs. State of Karnataka & Ors., (2000) 9 SCC 572
15. Selvi J. Jayalalitha Vs. State by Deputy Supdt. of Police reported in (2000) 9 SCC 754
16. Datla Krishnam Raju Vs. Excise Sub Inspector Kowtalam, A.P. (2000) 10 SCC 370
17. Kalyan Chandra Sarkar Versus Rajesh Ranjan alias Pappu Yadav & Anr. (2005) 3 SCC 284
18. Raj Kumar & Ors. Vs. Union of India & Anr. (2006) 1 SCC 737 at para 19
19. Union of India & Anr. Versus Shardindu (2007) 6 SCC 276 at para 33
20. "K" Judicial Officer reported in (2001) 3 SCC 54
21. Narpat Singh Etc. Etc. Vs. Jaipur Development Authority & Anr., (2002) 4 SCC 666
22. State of U.P. & Anr. Versus Johri Mal (2004) 4 SCC 714
23. Madhepura in a Tizzy Over Pappu Visit" in The Times of India dated 05.05.2004 (2004) 5 SCC 124
24. Y. Suresh Babu Versus State of A.P. & Anr., (2005) 1 SCC 347
25. Kalyan Chandra Sarkar Versus Rajesh Ranjan @ Pappu Yadav & Anr. (2005) 3 SCC 284

26. Mohd. Shamim & Ors. Versus Smt. Nahid Begum & Anr., (2005) 3 SCC 302
27. Jacob Mathew Versus State of Punjab & Anr., (2005) 6 SCC 1
28. G.M., O.N.G.C Ltd. Versus Sendhabhai Vastram Patel & Ors., (2005) 6 SCC 454
29. Harigovind Yadav Versus Rewa Sidhi Gramin Bank & Ors. (2006) 6 SCC 145
30. Raj Kumar & Ors. Versus Union of India & Anr., (2006) 1 SCC 737
31. Secretary, State of Karnataka & Ors. Versus Umadevi & Ors., (2006) 4 SCC 1
32. Employees' State Insurance Corporation & Ors. Versus Jardine Henderson Staff Association & Ors., (2006) 6 SCC 581
33. Gurpreet Singh Versus Union of India (2006) 8 SCC 457
34. Manish Ratan & Ors. Versus State of M.P. & Anr., (2007) 1 SCC 262
35. Bharat Sewa Sansthan Versus U.P. Electronics Corporation Limited (2007) 7 SCC 737
36. Central Bank of India & Ors. Versus Madan Chandra Brahma & Anr., (2007) 8 SCC 294
37. Sabita Shashank Singh Versus Shashank Shekhar Singh in T.P. (Civil) No. 908 of 2019
38. Rhea Chakraborty Versus The State of Bihar T.P. (Crl.) No.225 of 2020 [AIR 2020 SC 3826]

39. Shilpa Shailesh Versus Varun Sreenivasan reported in (2023) SCC OnLine SC 544f
40. Reshmi Shaw alias Gupta Versus Bidesh Kumar Gupta reported in (2024) SCC OnLine SC 556

THE PLENARY POWER OF THE HON'BLE SUPREME COURT OF INDIA UNDER ARTICLE 142 OF THE CONSTITUTION

The momentous and imperative provision under Article 142 of the Constitution plays a pivotal role in the Indian Constitution that provides the Hon'ble Supreme Court with an exceptional authority for the enforcement of its verdict and rulings. The said Article ensures that the Hon'ble Supreme Court may pass any decree or order necessary to deliver complete justice in a case that handles or adjudicates. The orders passed by the Hon'ble Supreme Court would be enforceable throughout the country. The Article 142 was presented to the Constituent Assembly for deliberation on 27th May, 1949. On the same day without any debate, the Article was approved with the consensus with a view to enabling the Hon'ble Supreme Court of India to possess full power to deliver complete justice for the sake of upholding judicial independence. As per clause (1) of Article 142, the Supreme Court can exercise its power to issue any decree or order for doing complete justice in any cause or the case pending before it. Such decree or order is enforceable throughout India as mandated by any law passed by the parliament. Clause (2) of Article 142 empowers the Supreme Court to make any order to secure the attendance of any person, the discovery or production of any documents or the investigation or any punishment of any contempt of itself subject to the provisions of any law made by the Parliament.

The Article 142 of the Constitution vests the Supreme Court a substantial discretionary power to be used in the circumstances where to deliver the "complete justice". In a case where laws are found to be inadequate or insufficient for the purpose of grant of relief, the Hon'ble Supreme Court can exercise its plenary power under Article 142 of the Constitution. The Supreme Court in exercise of its jurisdiction under Article 142 of the Constitution cannot pass any order which would be tantamount to supersede the substantive law applicable to the case or dehors the statutory provisions to deal with the subject matter of the case. Such constitutional powers in no way can be restrained by any statutory provisions. At the same time, the Supreme Court cannot exercise such power under Article 142 of the Constitution to ignore a specific provision prescribed under a statute. The plenary powers of the Supreme Court under Article 142 of the Constitution are inherent in the court and therefore, the plenary powers are used by the Hon'ble Supreme Court as a complementary to the powers to be used for the sake of complete justice between the parties and are also in the nature of supplementary powers for the sake of prevention of injustice. In the case of **Kalyan Chandra Sarkar Versus Rajesh Ranjan alias Pappu Yadav & Anr. (2005) 3 SCC 284** wherein a constitutional issue required the Supreme Court to prevent "clogging or obstruction of stream of justice". The relevant paragraphs 26, 27, 32, 33 and 39 of the said judgment are reproduced as under:

"26. While it is true that this Court in exercise of its jurisdiction under Article 142 of the Constitution would not pass any order which would amount to supplanting substantive law applicable to the case or ignoring express statutory provisions dealing with the subject as has been held in Supreme Court Bar Assn. v. Union of India but it is useful to note the following : (SCC p. 432, para 48)

27. It may therefore be understood that the plenary powers of this Court under Article 142 of the Constitution are inherent in the Court and are complementary to those powers which are specifically conferred on the Court by various statutes though are not limited by those statutes. These powers also exist independent of the statutes with a view to do complete justice between the parties ... and are in the nature of supplementary powers ... (and) may be put on a different and perhaps even wider footing than ordinary inherent powers of a court to prevent injustice. The advantage that is derived from a constitutional provision couched in such a wide compass is that it prevents "clogging or obstruction of the stream of

justice." (See Supreme Court Bar Assn., SCC p. 431, para 47.)

32. Article 142 vests the Supreme Court with a repository of discretionary power that can be wielded in appropriate circumstances to deliver "complete" justice in a given case. Only Bangladesh (Article 104) and Nepal [Article 88(2)] include similar provisions in their Constitutions.

33. Article 142 is an important constitutional power granted to this Court to protect the citizens. In a given situation when laws are found to be inadequate for the purpose of grant of relief, the Court can exercise its jurisdiction under Article 142 of the Constitution. In Ashok Kumar Gupta v. State of U.P. (SCC at p. 250, para 60) this Court held:

"The phrase 'complete justice' engrafted in Article 142(1) is the word of width couched with elasticity to meet myriad situations created by human ingenuity or cause or result of operation of statute law or law declared under Articles 32, 136 and 141 of the Constitution...."

39. Finally as observed from the decisions in Vishaka v. State of Rajasthan and Vineet Narain v. Union of India directions issued by this Court under Article 142 form the law of the land in the absence of any substantive law covering that field. Such directions "fill the vacuum" until the legislature enacts substantive law."

The powers under Article 142 of the Constitution are meant to prevent any obstruction to the stream of justice and to supplement the existing legal framework to do the complete justice between the parties but not to supplant it. The concept and the necessity of this article are to meet the situations which cannot be effectively and suitably resolved by the existing provisions of law. The Supreme Court in exercise of its jurisdiction under Article 142 can grant appropriate relief where there is some apparent illegality or where there is a manifest want of jurisdiction or some palpable and express injustice for the sake of complete justice in any cause or matter. In this regard, the Supreme Court in the case of **Union of India & Anr. Versus Shardindu (2007) 6 SCC 276 at para 33** has held as under:

"Lastly, learned Additional Solicitor General submitted that Article 142 of the Constitution should be exercised in the present case as there is no such provision for the contingency which has arisen in the matter and the termination of the respondent should be upheld. In this connection, our attention was invited to a decision of this Court in Supreme Court Bar Assn. v. Union of India. This was a case where their Lordships exercised the inherent power under Article 142 of the Constitution. The Constitution Bench held that this Court in exercise of power under Article 142 of the Constitution cannot ignore any substantive statutory provision dealing with the subject. It is a residuary power, supplementary and complementary to the powers specifically conferred on the Supreme Court by statutes in order to do so. It is only intended to prevent any obstruction to the stream of justice. None of such contingencies exist in the present case so as to invoke the power under Article 142 of the Constitution. This case stands reaffirmed in Textile Labour Assn. v. Official Liquidator."

In a Criminal Contempt Case **in re : Vinay Chandra Mishra (1995) 2 SCC 584** the Hon'ble Supreme Court has held that the Supreme Court is bound to discharge its constitutional obligations whenever there is interference or obstruction to the courts of justice. In the said judgment the Hon'ble Supreme Court at paragraph 51 has held that the jurisdiction and powers of the Hon'ble Supreme Court under Article 142 which are supplementary in nature and are provided to do complete justice in any matter, are independent of the jurisdiction and powers of the Supreme Court under Article 129 which cannot be trammelled in any way by any statutory provisions including the provisions of the Advocates' Act, 1961 or the Contempt of Courts' Act, 1971. The Advocates' Act, 1961 has nothing to do with the contempt jurisdiction of the court including of the Supreme Court and the Contempt of Courts' Act, 1971 being a statute cannot denude, restrict or limit the powers of the Supreme Court to take action for contempt under Article 129.

The relevant parts of the said paragraph 51 are reproduced as under:

"What is further, the jurisdiction and powers of the Supreme Court under Article 142 which are supplementary in nature and are provided to do complete justice in any matter, are independent of the jurisdiction and powers of the Supreme Court under Article 129 which cannot be trammeled in any way by any statutory provision including the provision of the Advocates' Act or the Contempt of Courts' Act."

"There is no restriction or limitation on the nature of punishment that the Supreme Court may award while exercising its contempt jurisdiction and the said punishments can be the punishments. The Supreme Court may impose while exercising the said jurisdiction."

In addition to the observations in paragraph 51 of the above judgment, the Hon'ble Supreme Court has also observed in paragraph 46 of the said judgment that the jurisdiction of the Supreme Court under Article 129 is independent of the statutory law of contempt enacted by the parliament under Entry 77 of List – I of the Seventh Schedule of the Constitution. The relevant paragraphs 45 & 46 of the said judgment are reproduced as under:

"45. The question now is what punishment should be meted out to the contemner. We have already discussed the contempt jurisdiction of this Court under

Article 129 of the Constitution. That jurisdiction is independent of the statutory law of contempt enacted by Parliament under Entry 77 of List I of Seventh Schedule of the Constitution. The jurisdiction to take cognizance of the contempt as well as to award punishment for it being constitutional, it cannot be controlled by any statute. Neither, therefore, the Contempt of Courts Act, 1971 nor the Advocates Act, 1961 can be pressed into service to restrict the said jurisdiction. We had, during the course of the proceedings indicated that if we convict the contemner of the offence, we may also suspend his licence to practice as a lawyer. The learned counsel for the contemner and the interveners and also the learned Solicitor General appointed amicus curiae to assist the Court were requested to advance their arguments also on the said point. Pursuant to it, it was sought to be contended on behalf of the contemner and the U.P. Bar Association and the U.P. Bar Council that the Court cannot suspend the licence which is a power entrusted by the Advocates Act, 1961 specially made for the purpose, to thee disciplinary committees of the State Bar Councils and of the Bar Council of India. The argument was that even the constitutional power under Articles 129 and 142 was circumscribed by the said statutory provisions and hence in the exercise of our power under the said provisions, the licence of an advocate was not liable either to be cancelled or suspended. A reference was made in this connection to the provisions of Sections 35 and 36 of the Advocates

Act, which show that the power to punish the advocate is vested in the disciplinary committees of the State Bar Councils and the Bar Council of India. Under Section 37 of the Advocates Act, an appeal lies to the Bar Council of India, when the order is passed by the disciplinary committee of the State Bar Council. Under Section 38, the appeal lies to this Court when the order is made by the disciplinary committee of the Bar Council of India, either under Section 36 or in appeal under Section 37. The power to punish includes the power to suspend the advocate from practice for such period as the disciplinary committee concerned may deem fit under Section 35(3)(c) and also to remove the name of the advocate from the State roll of the Advocates under Section 35(3)*(d)*. Relying on these provisions, it was contended that since the Act has vested the powers of suspending and removing the advocate from practice exclusively in the disciplinary committees of the State Bar Councils and the Bar Council of India, as the case may be, the Supreme Court is denuded of its power to impose such punishment both under Articles 129 and 142 of the Constitution. In support of this contention, reliance was placed on the observations of the majority of this Country in *Prem Chand Garg v. Excise Commr., U.P.* relating to the powers of this Court under Article 142 which are as follows:

"In this connection, it may be pertinent to point out that the wide powers which are given to this Court for doing complete justice between the parties, can be used by this Court for instance, in adding parties to the proceedings pending before it, or in admitting additional evidence, or in remanding the case, or in allowing a new point to be taken for the first time. It is plain that in exercising these and similar other powers, this Court would not be bound by the relevant provisions of procedure if it is satisfied that a departure from the said procedure is necessary to do complete justice between the parties.

That takes us to the second argument urged by the Solicitor General that Article 142 and Article 32 should be reconciled by the adoption of the rule of harmonious construction. *In this connection, we ought to bear in mind that though the powers conferred on this Court by Article 142(1) are very wide, and the same can be exercised for doing complete justice in any case, as we have already observed, this Court cannot even under Article 142(1) make an order plainly inconsistent with the express statutory provisions of substantive law, much less, inconsistent with any constitutional provisions. There can, therefore, be no conflict between Article 142(1) and Article 32. In the case of K.M. Nanavati v. State of Bombay* on which the Solicitor General relies, it was conceded, and rightly, that under Article 142(1) this Court had the power to grant bail in cases brought before it, and so, there was obviously a conflict between the power vested in this Court under the said

Article and that vested in the Governor of the State under Article 161. The possibility of a conflict between these powers necessitated the application of the rule of harmonious construction. The said rule can have no application to the present case, because on a fair construction of Article 142(1), this Court has no power to circumscribe the fundamental right guaranteed under Article 32. The existence of the said power is itself in dispute, and so, the present case is clearly distinguishable from the case of *K.M. Nanavati.*"

"46. Apart from the fact that these observations are made with reference to the powers of this Court under Article 142 which are in the nature of supplementary powers and not with reference to this Court's power under Article 129, the said observations have been explained by this Court in its later decisions in *Delhi Judicial Service Assn. v. State of Gujarat* and *Union Carbide Corpn. v. Union of India.* In para 51 of the former decision, it has been, with respect, rightly pointed out that the said observations were made with regard to the extent of this Court's power under Article 142(1) in the context of fundamental rights. Those observations have no bearing on the present issue. No doubt, it was further observed there that those observations have no bearing on the question in issue in that case as there was no provision in any substantive law restricting this Court's power to quash proceedings pending before subordinate courts. But it was also added there that this Court's power under Article 142(1) to do complete justice was entirely of a different level and of a different quality. Any prohibition or restriction contained in ordinary laws cannot act as a limitation on the constitutional power of this Court. Once this Court is in seisin of a matter before it, it has power to issue any order or direction to do complete justice in the matter. A reference was made in that connection to the concurring opinion of Justice A.N. Sen in *Harbans Singh* v. *State of U.P.* where the learned Judge observed as follows: (SCC pp. 107-08, para 20).

"Very wide powers have been conferred on this Court for due and proper administration of justice. Apart from the jurisdiction and powers conferred on this Court under Articles 32 and 136 of the Constitution, I am of the opinion that this Court retains and must retain, an inherent power and jurisdiction for dealing with any extraordinary situation in the larger interests of administration of justice and for preventing manifest injustice being done. This power must necessarily be sparingly used only in exceptional circumstances for furthering the ends of justice."

The Court has then gone on to observe there that no enactment made by Central or State legislature can limit or restrict the power of this Court under Article 142 of the Constitution, though the Court must take into consideration the statutory provisions regulating the matter in dispute. What would be the need of complete justice in a cause or matter, would depend upon the facts and circumstances of each case."

Relying upon the above mentioned judgment i.e. Vinay Chandra Mishra case, the Hon'ble Supreme Court subsequently in the case of **Delhi Development Authority Versus Skipper Construction Company (P) Ltd. & Anr., (1996) 4 SCC 622** has taken a view on doing complete justice between the parties by exercising the power under Article 142 of the Constitution. The relevant parts of paragraph 16, 17, 19 and 21 of the said judgment are reproduced as under:

"The power under Article 142 is meant to supplement the existing legal framework – to do complete justice between the parties – and not to supplant it. It is conceived to meet situations which cannot be effectively and appropriately tackled by the existing provisions of law. As a matter of fact, we think it advisable to leave this power undefined and uncatalogued so that it remains elastic enough to be moulded to suit the given situation. The very fact that this power is conferred only upon this Court, and on no one else, is itself an assurance that it will be used with due restraint and circumspection, keeping in view the ultimate object of doing complete justice between the parties."

(Para 16)

"Where an act is done in violation of an order of stay or injunction, it is the duty of the court, as a policy, to set the wrong right and not allow the perpetuation of the wrongdoing. The principle that a contemnor ought not to be permitted to enjoy and/or keep the fruits of his contempt is well settled. Undergoing the punishment for contempt does not mean that the court is not entitled to give appropriate directions for remedying and rectifying the things done in violation of its orders. The inherent power of the court is not only available in such a case, but it is bound to exercise it to undo the wrong in the interest of justice. This salutory rule has to be applied and given effect to by the Supreme Court, if necessary, by overruling any procedural or other technical objections. Article 129 is a constitutional power and when exercised in tandem with Article 142, all such objections should give way. The court must ensure full justice between the parties before it."

(Para 17, 19 & 21)

The Hon'ble Supreme Court under Article 142 can exercise the plenary and residuary powers under Article 32 and 136 of the Constitution for the sake of quashing criminal proceedings pending before any court. In this regard the Supreme Court in the case of Delhi Judicial Service Association Versus State of Gujarat (1991) 4 SCC 406 may be referred. The Supreme Court has also in the case of **Consumer Education and Research Centre Versus Union of**

India & Ors., (1995) 3 SCC 42 at para 28 held on the basis of the facts of that case that in an appropriate case, the court would give appropriate directions to the employer, be it that State or its undertaking or private employer to make the right to life meaningful to prevent pollution of workplace, protection of environment, protection of health of the workman or to preserve free and unpolluted water for the safety and health of the people. The authorities or even the private persons or industry are bound by the directions issued by the Supreme Court under Article 32 and Article 142 of the Constitution.

However, at the same time, the power of the Hon'ble Supreme Court under Article 142 of the Constitution may be or it cannot be used to grant a relief where a question arises not falling within its jurisdiction under this Article. In this regard the Hon'ble Supreme Court in the case of State of Karnataka Versus State of Andhra Pradesh & Ors. (2000) 9 SCC 572 at paragraph 60 has held that the jurisdiction of the court in a suit under Article 131 of the Constitution is quite wide as apparent from the language used in the said Article and as has been interpreted by the Hon'ble Supreme Court in the said judgment relied upon the cases in the matter of **State of Karnataka Versus Union of India (1977) 4 SCC 608** and **State of Rajasthan Versus Union of India (1977) 3 SCC 592**. It is relevant to state that in the paragraph 60 of the above mentioned judgment i.e. State of Karnataka

Versus State of Andhra Pradesh (2000) 9 SCC 572, the Hon'ble Supreme Court has observed as under:

"**60.** It is no doubt true that the jurisdiction of the Court in a suit under Article 131 of the Constitution is quite wide, which is apparent from the language used in the said article and as has been interpreted by this Court in the two cases already referred to (see State of Karnataka case and State of Rajasthan case). It is also true that Article 142 confers wide powers on this Court to do complete justice between the parties and the Court can pass any order or issue any direction that may be necessary, but at the same time, within the meaning of Article 131, the dispute that has been raised in the present suit is between the State of Andhra Pradesh and the State of Karnataka and question, therefore, would be whether it involves any existence or extent of a legal right of such dispute. In answering such a dispute, it may be difficult to entertain a further dispute on the question of submergence as raised by the State of Maharashtra, a co-defendant. But in view of the stand taken by Mr. Nariman, without further delving into the matter and without expressing any final opinion, whether such a stand, as the one taken by Maharashtra is possible for being adjudicated upon, we would examine the merits of the said contention. A bare perusal of the report of the Tribunal setting out the facts as found by it and giving its decision on the matters referred to it as per Exh.PK 1 as well as the further report of the said

Tribunal, giving explanation to the application for clarifications filed by the different States, as per Exh.PK 2, we find that the question of submergence within the territory of the State of Maharashtra on account of Almatti Dam in the State of Karnataka has not at all been discussed nor any opinion has been expressed thereon. The Tribunal having given its decision on the question of sharing of the water in River Krishna on en bloc allocation basis, if the user of such water in a particular way, becomes detrimental to another State, then such a grievance would be a fresh dispute within the meaning of Section 2(c) read with Section 3 of the Act and it cannot be held to be an adjudicated dispute of the Tribunal. We have already indicated that it is only an adjudicated dispute between the States on which a decision has been given by a tribunal constituted under Section 4 of the Act by the Government of India, that can be a subject-matter of a suit under Article 131, if there is any breach in implementation of the said decision of the tribunal. But a dispute between the two States in relation to the said inter-State river arising out of the user of the water by one State would be a fresh water dispute and as such would be barred under Article 262 read with Section 11 of the Inter-State Water Disputes Act, 1956. The question of submergence of land pursuant to the user of water in respect of an inter-State river allocated in favour of a particular State is inextricably connected with the allocation of water itself and the present grievance of the State of Maharashtra would be a complaint on account of an executive action of the State of Karnataka within the meaning of Section 3(a) and also would be a water dispute within the ambit of Section 2(c) and, therefore, it would not be appropriate for this Court to entertain and examine and answer the same. We do appreciate the concern of the State of Maharashtra, when it comes to its knowledge that there would be large-scale inundation and submergence of its territory if the height of Almatti Dam is allowed to be raised to 524.256 metres, as per the latest project report of the State of Karnataka, but such concern of the State of Maharashtra alone would not be sufficient for this Court to decide the matter and issue any order of injunction as prayed for in the additional written statement filed by the State of Maharashtra and on the other hand, it would be a matter for being agitated upon before a tribunal to be constituted by the Government of India in the event a complaint is made to that effect by the State of Maharashtra. We also do not find sufficient materials in this proceeding before us to enable this Court to come to a positive conclusion as to what would be the effect on the question of submergence, if the height of the dam at Almatti is allowed to be constructed up to 524.256 metres inasmuch as, according to the State of Maharashtra, the joint surveys are still on. It is too well settled that no court can issue an order of mandatory injunction on mere apprehension without positive data about the adverse effects being placed and without any definite conclusion on the question of irreparable injury and balance of convenience. Then again, while allowing a particular State to use the water of an inter-State river, if the manner of such user really submerges some land in some other State, then the question has to be gone into as to what would be the amount of compensation and how the question of rehabilitation of those persons within the submerged area can be dealt with which really is an aspect of the doctrine of equitable apportionment and all these can be gone into, if a complaint regarding the same is made and the Government of India appoints a tribunal for the said purpose. But these things cannot be gone into, in a suit filed under Article 131 as a part of implementation of an adjudicated dispute of a tribunal. It is also surprising to note that even though the original project report of 1970 in relation to Almatti Dam had been produced before the Tribunal, which was adjudicating the disputes raised by different States, yet the State of Maharashtra never thought of the question of submergence and never attempted to get that question decided upon. In the aforesaid premises, howsoever wide the power of the Court under Article 142 of the Constitution may be, we do not think it proper to entertain the question of submergence, raised by the State of Maharashtra in its additional written statement and decide the question of injunction, in relation to the height of Almatti Dam on that basis. Issue 9(c) is accordingly decided against the State of Maharashtra."

In the case of **M/s Essar Constructions Versus M.P. Ramakrishna Reddy (2000) 6 SCC 94** the factual position was that the High Court had decided a revision petition whereas an appeal lay and should have been filed, it was held to be an appropriate case to be decided by the Supreme Court on merits instead of remitting to the High Court for fresh decision after treating it as an appeal.

From the cases cited hereinabove, it is crystal clear that the framers of the Constitution have given an extraordinary power to the Supreme Court under Article 142 to mould the relief by safeguarding the interest of the litigants. The paramount consideration in the cases where the justice has to be done for ensuring the justice to avoid injustice. In this regard the Supreme Court in the case of **Raj Kumar & Ors. Versus Union of India & Anr., (2006) 1 SCC 737 at para 19** has held that having regard to the peculiar facts of the case, directions be issued in exercise of its powers under Article 142 of the Constitution of India in order to do complete justice to a section of the personnel who would otherwise be placed inequitable situation for which the authorities are also partly to blame. It is open to the Hon'ble Supreme Court to mould the relief by safeguarding the interests of the parties even while declaring the law. The paramount consideration in such cases should be to ensure that there is no injustice caused. Barring this limited relief, no other relief is due to the Petitioners before the Hon'ble Supreme Court.

As per the 'Advanced Law Lexicon' dictionary, plenary power means the power that is broadly construed especially a court's power to dispose of any matter properly before it. Article 142 of the Constitution of India contemplates that the Supreme Court in the exercise of its jurisdiction may pass such decree or make such order as is necessary for doing complete justice in any cause or matter pending before it, and any decree so passed or order so made shall be enforceable throughout the territory of India in such manner as may be prescribed by or under any law made by Parliament and until provision in that behalf is so made in such manner as the President may by order prescribe. It is further contemplated under sub-clause (2) of the said Article that subject to the provision of any law made on this behalf by the Parliament, the Supreme Court shall in respect of the whole of the territory of India, has got all and every power to make any order for the purpose of securing the attendance of any person, the discovery or production of any documents, or the investigation or punishment of any contempt of itself. Taking into account the facts as narrated in the case of **Pt. Shamboo Nath Tikoo & Ors. Versus S. Gian Singh & Ors., (1995) Supp. 3 SCC 266**, the Hon'ble Supreme Court substantially has held exercising the power under Articles 142 and 132 of the Constitution as under:

"Suit for ejectment and recovery of possession – Sikhs, defendant-respondents having no right to two rooms (converted into three rooms) in the Southern Dharamshalla of Martand Shrine in Anantnag District in J&K where they are keeping their Granth Sahib either on ground of grant made by the then ruler Maharaja Pratap Singh or on ground of their perfecting title thereto by adverse possession – Sikhs, defendants, also having no right to two rooms (converted into three rooms) in the Southern Dharamshalla of Martand Shrine in Anantnag District in J&K where they are keeping their Granth Sahib either on ground of grant made by the then ruler Maharaja Pratap Singh or on ground of grant made by the then ruler Maharaja Pratap Singh or on ground of their perfecting title thereto by adverse possession – Sikhs, defendants, also having no right to hold Dewans on three specific occasions of the year in the open space of the Martand Shrine towards Pahalgam Road – However, on facts, in the interest of justice held, there is no warrant for ordering ejectment of the defendant-respondents from the said room or restraining them by permanent injunction from holding Dewans in the said open space – This is subject to liability of the defendants for ejectment from the said rooms if they misuse their permissive possession under which they are allowed to continue in those rooms and of the liability of the defendants to be restrained from using the open space to hold Dewans on three occasions every year, if they or their men misuse the permission to hold such Dewans now granted by indulging in acts that would cause obstruction or annoyance to Hindus in performance of their pujas or conducting religious ceremonies in the precincts of their own Martand Shrine and springs therein – Constitution of India, Arts. 142 and 132".

(Paras 23, 31, 40, 47 to 51)

(Coram: Hon'ble Mr. Justice K. Ramaswamy & Hon'ble Mr. Justice N. Venkatachala)

The Hon'ble Supreme Court in the case of **C. Chenga Reddy and Others Versus State of A.P. (1996) 10 SCC 193** exercising the power under Article 142 of the Constitution has held at paragraph 56 as under:

"A court of equity must so act, within the permissible limits so as to prevent injustice. "Equity is not past the age of child-bearing" and an effort to do justice between the parties is a compulsion of judicial conscience. Courts can and should strive to evolve an appropriate remedy, in the facts and circumstances of a given case, so as to further the cause of justice, within the available range and forging new tools for the said purpose, if necessary to chisel hard edges of the law.

In view of the findings with regard to the violation of the codal provisions and administrative lapses by the departmental officials, a departmental enquiry may be justified but in this fact-situation, it would be an unnecessary exercise. The counsel for the delinquent officers (appellants) have been heard by the Supreme Court at length and they were unable to assail the findings of the courts below regarding codal violations and administrative lapses which may have caused some loss to the exchequer also. In the established facts and circumstances of these cases, it would be appropriate with a view to do complete justice between the parties, in exercise of jurisdiction under Article 142 of the Constitution of India, to direct that no departmental enquiry shall now be initiated against the departmental officials for their established administrative breaches and violation of the codal provisions in 1979-80. Consequent upon their acquittal, the officials shall be reinstated in service with continuity of service for all purposes but for their established administrative lapses and breach of codal provisions etc., they shall not be entitled to any back wages or any other type of monetary benefit for the period they remained out of service. The suspension allowance, if any, received by all or any one of them shall however not be recovered from them. This punishment appears to be commensurate with the gravity of their lapses and shall serve the ends of justice. Those of the officials who may have reached the age of superannuation in the meanwhile, will get their pensionary benefits calculated on the basis of their continuous service but they shall be entitled to draw pension with effect from the date of this order only." **(Para 56)**

(Coram: Hon'ble Mr. Justice G.N. Ray & Hon'ble Dr. Justice A.S. Anand)

The Hon'ble Supreme Court exercising its power under Article 142 of the Constitution in the case of **Selvi J. Jayalalitha Vs. State by Deputy Supdt. of Police reported in (2000) 9 SCC 754** and thereby the appellant was given opportunities to present the defence evidence or to produce the list of defence witnesses. While granting such opportunities, the Hon'ble Supreme Court at para 4 was pleased to observe as under:

"True, the appellant was given opportunities to present the defence evidence or to produce the list of defence witnesses and the appellant has not availed herself of those opportunities. Yet as a court of justice we are of the view that one more opportunity can be granted to the appellant for examining the defence witnesses if she proposes to do."

The scope of the Article 142 has been considered in various decisions. In one of the judgments of the Hon'ble Supreme Court i.e. **Supreme Court Bar Association Versus Union of India & Anr., (1998) 4 SCC 409**, the Supreme Court has held that the plenary powers under Article 142 of the Constitution are inherent in the court and are complimentary to those powers which are specifically conferred on the court by various statutes, though are not limited by those statutes. These statutory powers are also independent in nature with a view to do complete justice between the parties. Such plenary powers stand upon foundation and the basis of its exercise may be put on a different and perhaps even wider footing to prevent injustice in the process of litigation and to do a complete justice between the parties. The plenary power is, therefore, plays a substantial role as the residual source of power which the Supreme Court may draw upon or exercise it as necessary whenever it is just equitable to do so to ensure to do complete justice between the parties. The Hon'ble Supreme Court has, therefore, held in the said judgment is that the Article 142 is an indispensible adjunct to all other powers and is free from the restraint of jurisdiction and operates as a valuable weapon in the hands of the Supreme Court to prevent "clogging or obstruction of the scheme of justice".

In a contempt proceedings In Re: **Vinay Chandra Mishra reported in (1995) 2 SCC 584** stated supra, the Hon'ble Supreme Court exercising the power under Article 129 read with Article 142 of the Constitution in the light of the facts and circumstances of the case was pleased to justify the sentence for the conviction of the Petitioner for committing the criminal contempt stated at paragraph 55 of the judgment reproduced as under:

"55. The facts and circumstances of the present case justify our invoking the power under Article 129 read with Article 142 of the Constitution to award to the contemnor a suspended sentence of imprisonment together with suspension of his practice as an advocate in the manner directed herein. We accordingly sentence the contemnor for his conviction for the offence of criminal contempt as under:

(a) The contemnor Vinay Chandra Mishra is hereby sentenced to undergo simple imprisonment for a period of six weeks. However, in the circumstances of the case, the sentence will remain suspended for a period of four years and may be activated in case the contemnor is convicted for any other offence of contempt of court within the said period; and

(b) The contemnor shall stand suspended from practicing as an advocate for a period of three years from today with the consequence that all elective and nominated offices/posts at present held by him in his capacity as an advocate, shall stand vacated by him forthwith."

However, the Hon'ble Supreme Court in the subsequent judgment stated hereinabove i.e. in Supreme Court Bar Association case, was pleased to take a different view between Article 129 and Article 142 and thereby partly overruled the Vinay Chandra Mishra case. In the said case the Hon'ble Supreme Court relied upon its appellate jurisdiction under

Section 38 of the Advocates' Act, 1961 and supported its order suspending the license of the contemner (the Petitioner V.C. Mishra). The Hon'ble Supreme Court is indeed the final appellate authority under Section 38 of the Advocates' Act, 1961 but it is not possible to agree with the view taken by the Hon'ble Supreme Court that the Hon'ble Supreme Court can exercise of its appellate jurisdiction under Section 38 of the Act that while punishing a contemnor Advocate in a contempt case. The delinquent Advocate may be suspended from practice for a specified period or even removed from the rolls of the Advocates or imposed any other punishment as provided under the Act. The enquiry is a detailed and elaborate one and is not of a summary nature. It is, therefore, not permissible for the Hon'ble Supreme Court to punish an Advocate for the professional "misconduct" in exercise of the appellate jurisdiction by converting itself as a statutory body exercising original jurisdiction. The Hon'ble Supreme Court may well have the jurisdiction in exercise of its appellate powers under Section 38 of the Act read with Article 142 of the Constitution to proceed suo-motu and send for records from the Bar Council and pass appropriate orders against the Advocates concerned. In an appropriate case, the Hon'ble Supreme Court may exercise the appellate jurisdiction even suo-motu provided there is some cause pending before the concerned Bar Council and the Bar Council does not act or fails to act by sending for record of that cause and pass appropriate orders.

The dual jurisdictions are separate and different in nature. It is, therefore, not possible to subscribe to the contrary view expressed by the bench in V.C. Mishra's case because in that case, the Bar Council had not declined to deal with the matter and take appropriate action against the Advocate concerned. In that case since there was no cause pending before the Bar Council, the Hon'ble Supreme Court could not exercise its appellate jurisdiction in respect of a matter which was never under consideration of the Bar Council. It must, therefore, be held that Hon'ble Supreme Court cannot in the exercise of its jurisdiction under Article 142 read with Article 129 of the Constitution while punishing a contemnor for committing contempt of court also imposed a punishment of suspending the license of the Advocate concerned. Such a punishment cannot even be imposed by taking recourse to the appellate powers under Section 38 of the Act while dealing with a case of contempt of court. Section 38 of the Advocates' Act, 1961 contemplates as under:

"**38. Appeal to the Supreme Court.-** Any person aggrieved by an order made by the disciplinary committee of the Bar Council of India under section 36 or section 37 [or the Attorney-General of India or the Advocate-General of the State concerned, as the case may be,] may within sixty days of the date on which the order is communicated to him, prefer an appeal to the Supreme Court and the Supreme Court may pass such order [(including an order varying the punishment awarded by the disciplinary committee of the Bar Council of India)] thereon as it deems fit:

[Provided that no order of the disciplinary committee of the Bar Council of India shall be varied by the Supreme Court so as to prejudicially affect the person aggrieved without giving him a reasonable opportunity of being heard.]"

To that extent, the law laid down in Vinay Chandra Mishra case, re: is not a good law and the same was overruled. Article 129 contemplates that the Supreme Court shall be a court of record and shall have all the powers of such a court including the power to punish for contempt of itself. At the same time, the Constitution has vested the plenary power under Article 142 of the Constitution to be used as complementary to meet the ends of justice. The said Article contemplates that in exercise of the jurisdiction, the Hon'ble Supreme Court may pass such decree or make such order as is necessary for doing complete justice in any case or matter pending before it and any decree so passed or order so made shall be enforceable throughout the territory of India in such a manner as may be prescribed by or under any law made by Parliament and until such provision in that behalf is so made in such a manner as the President may by order prescribe. In the case of **M.C. Mehta Versus Kamal Nath & Ors., (2000) 6 SCC 213** the Hon'ble Supreme Court has held that the power under Article 142 cannot be exercised by Hon'ble Supreme Court where the issue can be settled through substantive provisions of statutes. The Hon'ble Supreme Court in some cases considering the prolonged suffering from mental torture, agony due to imprisonment has exercised the plenary power under Article 142 of the Constitution. In the case of **Datla Krishnam Raju Vs. Excise Sub Inspector Kowtalam, A.P. (2000) 10 SCC 370**, the Hon'ble Supreme Court has reduced the sentence below the statutory minimum punishment after considering the special facts and circumstances warranting such reduction by its order dated 3rd February 1999. The content of the said order is reproduced as under:

"The appellant has been convicted under Section 34(a) of the Andhra Pradesh Excise Act (for short "the Act") for having been found in possession of arrack beyond the permissible limit under Section 18 (sic 14) of the said Act. The Magistrate as well as the learned Sessions Judge in appeal and the High Court in revision have concurrently come to the conclusion that the appellant was in possession of the intoxicant in question. Mrs. Amareswari, learned Senior Counsel appearing for the appellant, however, relying upon the two Single-Judge judgments of the Andhra Pradesh High Court in Boya Urukondamma v. State of A.P. and Mohd. Ghousuddin v. State of A.P. contends that mere possession will not constitute an offence under Section 34(a) and the prosecution must establish that such possession was either for import, export, transport or manufacture. The two Single-Judge decisions undoubtedly, support the contention of the learned counsel for the appellant but in the impugned judgment the Division Bench of the High Court has reversed the decision of the aforesaid two Single-Judge Bench decisions and has come to the conclusion that possession beyond the prescribed limit would constitute an offence under Section 34(a) of the Act. Having examined the provisions of Section 34(a) and Section 34(h) and the special language used therein the conclusion is that mere possession beyond the prescribed limit will constitute an offence and therefore the conclusion of the High Court cannot be found fault with. In view of the finding of the forums below that the appellant was found in possession of the intoxicants beyond the prescribed limit it must be held that he has committed offence under Section 34(a) of the Act. Once conviction is under Section 34(a) of the Act, the statute prescribes a minimum punishment of six months. The learned counsel for the appellant states that the occurrence itself is of the year 1989 and the appellant has already undergone the sentence for a period of 45 days and taking into account the fact that the two earlier decisions were operating it would not be necessary to direct the appellant to surrender for serving the balance period of sentence. We are persuaded to accept this contention, particularly, when more than ten years have elapsed since the date of occurrence and, therefore, the sentence is reduced to the period already undergone i.e. to the extent of 45 days and with a fine of Rs.5000, failing which the appellant shall undergo imprisonment for a period of five months. The fine should be paid within five months. We make it clear that we are reducing the sentence in this case in view of the special facts and circumstances of the present case. The appeal is, thus, disposed of."

In the light of the facts and circumstances of a case in the matter of **Narpat Singh Etc. Etc. Vs. Jaipur Development Authority & Anr., (2002) 4 SCC 666**, the Hon'ble Supreme Court exercised the power under Article 142 of the Constitution of India to do the complete justice in that case and not to leave the appellants in the lurch although the Hon'ble Supreme Court had the power under Article 136 of the Constitution to consider the case which is discretionary in nature. The relevant paragraphs 7, 8, 10, 11 and 12 are reproduced as under:

"7. It is clear from the counter-affidavit filed on behalf of the respondents, and which fact has not been disputed on behalf of the appellants, that while the land acquired from the appellants was uncultivated fallow land with no well, superstructure or habitat built thereon, what has been offered to each of them is a developed plot of 1000 or 2000 square yard area. A developed plot of 1000 or 2000 square yards means at least 1500 or 3000 square yards of undeveloped land which is more than the area which has been acquired from them. The concept behind allotting residential plots to the persons whose land has been acquired is to rehabilitate them and to give some relief on reasonable terms because of their having been expropriated by land acquisition proceedings. So far as the appellants are concerned, the allotment of plots cannot be said to have fulfilled the object of rehabilitating them because though they lost their land but there is no material placed on record to hold them as having been rendered destitute on account of either their residence or their livelihood having been lost on account of land acquisition proceedings.

8. Secondly, during the course of hearing Shri G.L. Sanghi, Senior Advocate assisted by Shri S.K. Bhattacharyya, the learned counsel for the respondents, extensively read the decisions of this Court in the cases of Radhey Shyam and Daulat Mal Jain, in particular the latter one wherein this Court has noticed blatant misuse of power having been made by the holders of public office, bureaucrats and unscrupulous beneficiaries having combined together and depriving the State of its valuable land going to the extent of defeating the very public purpose for which acquisitions were made and plots having been allotted to powerful or affluent persons. The judgment in Daulat Mal Jain case makes a reference to the inquiry report dated 12-11-1992 of the Lokayukta of Rajasthan under Section 10 of the Rajasthan Lokayukta and Up-Lokayukta Act, 1973 wherein

prima facie finding has been recorded against the then Hon'ble Minister, Urban Development and Housing Department, Government of Rajasthan-cum-Chairman, JDA, the then Commissioner, JDA and the then Zonal Officer, Lal Kothi Scheme, having caused wrongful gain to themselves and wrongful loss to Jaipur Development Authority and the public at large by making allotments of residential plots. Shri G.L. Sanghi, the learned Senior Counsel produced for our perusal the inquiry report dated 12-11-1992 of the Lokayukta and read out extensively a few passages therefrom. The report makes a reference interalia to the land allotted to the 12 awardees including the four appellants herein, by way of compromise are out of the same land which was acquired for public purpose and out of which other allotments made were struck down by this Court in Daulat Mal Jain case.

10. Without entering into the question whether it is permissible for the Land Acquisition Officer or the Reference Court or the High Court hearing an appeal against an award made by the Reference Court to record a compromise where under the beneficiary of land acquisition agrees to offer land in lieu of monetary compensation and whether such a compromise would be legal and not opposed to public policy, we are of the opinion that the facts and circumstances of this case are enough to decline exercise of jurisdiction by this Court under Article 136 of the Constitution to the appellants. The exercise of

jurisdiction conferred by Article 136 of the Constitution on this Court is discretionary. It does not confer a right to appeal on a party to litigation; it only confers a discretionary power of widest amplitude on this Court to be exercised for satisfying the demands of justice. On one hand, it is an exceptional power to be exercised sparingly, with caution and care and to remedy extraordinary situations or situations occasioning gross failure of justice; on the other hand, it is an overriding power where under the Court may generously step in to impart justice and remedy injustice. The facts and circumstances of this case as have already been set out do not inspire the conscience of this Court to act in the aid of the appellants. It would, in our opinion, meet the ends of justice, and the appellants too ought to feel satisfied, if monetary compensation based on the principles for assessment thereof in land acquisition cases is awarded and in addition they are given each a plot of reasonable size to rehabilitate themselves so as to meet the demands of reasonability and consistency.

11. For this reason the appeals are held liable to be dismissed. Still, in exercise of jurisdiction conferred by Article 142 of the Constitution, two directions are warranted for doing complete justice in the case and not to leave the appellants in the lurch – remediless. And those directions we hereby make. Firstly, the appeals preferred by the State Government in the Rajasthan High Court were disposed of in terms of the

compromise and the monetary compensation was reduced in consideration of the awardees having been allotted plots. As we are holding the compromise to be vitiated, it would be in the interest of justice that the appeals filed by the State Government are restored for hearing on merits. The High Court shall hear and decide the appeals appointing the quantum of monetary compensation excluding, from its consideration, the allotment of plots to the awardees. Secondly, though the allotment of 1000 and 2000 square yards of land in Lal Kothi Scheme as a term of the compromise has been set aside by the High Court, it is directed that each appellant shall be allotted a residential plot of an area about 250 square yards in some other scheme of JDA at the rates effective and applicable on 17-8-1971, the date on which the compromise was arrived at. Such allotment shall be made and possession given within a period of three months from today. This direction we make in order to maintain consistency and uniformity in as much as we find almost all the awardees having been allotted plots and similar directions were made by this Court also in Daulat Mal Jain case, vide para 31. In case of any dispute arising in the matter of allotment of plots in terms of this direction, we allow liberty to the parties to approach the High Court of Rajasthan and seek directions preferably by the same Bench which will be hearing the appeals against the award made by the Reference Court.

12. It was vehemently contended on behalf of the respondents that the allotment of plots forming part of the compromise should be sustained because the appellants have, in view of the plots having been allotted to them, followed by delivery of possession, alienated the plots or created third-party interest therein and they would be put to serious inconvenience or placed in an awkward situation as the third parties would be after them while the allotted plots are lost by them. We are not inclined to agree. If the appellants have just alienated the plots allotted to them then securing of such plots was their adventure for profit and not a need for rehabilitation. Then, though they may lose the plots but they would be getting monetary compensation, solatium and interest in lieu of the land of which they have been expropriated. This must satisfy them. It was also submitted that the policy decision dated 6-12-2001 of the State of Rajasthan recognizes encroachers being settled in other schemes of JDA and if the encroachers enjoy the patronage of the State Government, why not the appellants who should not be compared with encroachers who are law-breakers. We need not comment on the policy of the State Government recognizing an encroacher's right to allotment of land. It is the wisdom of the State and we are not aware whether the policy is guided by socially beneficial consideration of providing a roof over the head of the deprived and poor or is a politically motivated policy of appeasement. For our purpose the relevant consideration is the decision of

this Court directing allotment of 250 square yard plot elsewhere to some such allottees whose allotment of plots in Lal Kothi Scheme was not upheld and maintaining consistency therewith. Maybe some awardees unscrupulously or by connivance or collusion and by lapse of time have succeeded in retaining allotment of larger plots in this very Scheme but such arbitrary or unreasonable allotments cannot be cited as precedent in support of misguided plea of equality. The appellants' prayer for upholding the compromise-based allotment of plots or in the alternative, plots of lesser size being allotted out of the land acquired for this very Scheme cannot be entertained much less allowed as that would be to some extent destructive of the purpose of acquisition. The land acquired must be used for the public purpose for which it has been acquired."

When the Terrorist and Disruptive Activities (Prevention) Act, 1987 was prevailing, an appeal was heard by the Hon'ble Supreme Court titled as **Bonkya Alias Bharatshivaji Mane & Ors. Vs State of Maharashtra (1995) 6 SCC 447**, the Hon'ble Supreme Court held at para 23 of the said judgment as under:

"The amplitude of powers available to this Court under Article 142 of the Constitution of India is normally speaking not conditioned by any statutory provision but it cannot be lost sight of that this Court exercises jurisdiction under Article 142 of the

Constitution with a view to do justice between the parties but not in disregard of the relevant statutory provisions. The transfer of the appeal to the High Court, after hearing the appeal on merits and finding that Section 3 of TADA on the basis of the evidence led by the prosecution, was not made out, is neither desirable nor proper nor permissible let alone justified. There cannot be piecemeal hearing of an appeal on merits – first by this Court to determine if an offence under TADA is made out or not and then by the High Court. The submission of the learned counsel is, thus, devoid of merits and is consequently rejected."

In a case where the offence is non-compoundable under Section 320 of the Code of Criminal Procedure, 1973 the Hon'ble Supreme Court has exercised its power under Article 142 of the Constitution of India and making it binding under Article 141 of the Constitution of India by exercising the power under the vision of Article 142, the Hon'ble Supreme Court has compounded the offence under Section 326 of the Indian Penal Code considering the submission of the accused for settlement, the Hon'ble Court directed the Appellant/Petitioner to pay Rs.10,000/- to the Respondent No.2 (the injured) for setting aside the order of conviction and sentence passed by the trial court and affirmed by the concerned High Court i.e. in the case of **Y. Suresh Babu Versus State of A.P. & Anr., (2005) 1 SCC 347**. However, the Hon'ble Supreme Court made it clear that this case shall not be treated as precedent. The relevant paragraph 2 of the said order is reproduced as under:

"2. Taking an overall view of the facts and circumstances, we grant leave as a special case to the parties to compound the offence on condition that the appellant pays Rs.10,000 to Respondent 2 by way of compensation for the physical injury suffered by him. The amount of compensation shall be deposited in the Court of IInd Additional Metropolitan Sessions Judge, Hyderabad within one month from today. If the amount is not deposited within the period allowed, the conviction and sentence recorded by the courts below against the appellant under Section 326 of the Code shall stand. However, if the amount is deposited within the time allowed, the conviction and sentence of the appellant under Section 326 of the Indian Penal Code shall be set aside. Respondent 2 shall be at liberty to withdraw the said amount unconditionally. The appellant shall in the meanwhile be enlarged on bail by the learned IInd Additional Metropolitan Sessions Judge on such terms as he thinks fit. This case shall not be treated as a precedent."

The Supreme Court in the case of **Employees' State Insurance Corporation & Ors. Versus Jardine Henderson Staff Association & Ors., (2006) 6 SCC 581** has held that under Article 142 of the Constitution, it (the Supreme Court) is empowered to mould the relief in such a manner so that it is not only just but also equitable even while declaring the law. It has also been held by the Hon'ble Supreme Court, the court is empowered to mould the relief in such a manner so that it is not only just but also equitable even while declaring the law as observed in para 62 of the judgment by referring to the cases such as **G.M., O.N.G.C Ltd. Versus Sendhabhai Vastram Patel & Ors., (2005) 6 SCC 454** and **Raj Kumar Versus Union of India & Anr., (2006) 1 SCC 737**. The relevant paragraph 62 of the above mentioned judgment i.e. **Employees' State Insurance Corporation & Ors. Versus Jardine Henderson Staff Association & Ors., (2006) 6 SCC 581** is reproduced as under:

"62. This Court under Article 142 of the Constitution of India is empowered to pass such orders as would do complete justice between the parties. This Court is also empowered to mould the relief in such a manner so that it is not only just but also equitable even while declaring the law as observed in para 25 of *ONGC Ltd. v. Sendhabhai Vastram Patel and Raj Kumar v. Union of India.* It is also permissible in law to prospectively overrule a judgment as has been done recently in *SBP & Co. v. Patel Engg. Ltd.* If the appellant is now allowed to recover from the erstwhile covered employees, it would severely affect industrial relations. Reversal of the impugned order would lead to prosecution, penalty and also interest against the respondents without any fault of the respondents. The decision of this Court in ITDC Employees' Union is clearly distinguishable as unlike in the present case, in that case, the High Court did not give any positive direction. The decision of the High Court was not reversed by this Court."

It is pertinent to mention here that the Hon'ble Supreme Court has categorically held in the case of **State of U.P. & Anr. Versus Johri Mal (2004) 4 SCC 714** while comparing the power of the High Court under Article 226 and that of the Supreme Court of India under Article 142 of the Constitution that the power under Article 226 is not at par with Article 142 of the Constitution. The relevant paragraph 57 of the said judgment is reproduced as under:

"The High Court failed to consider that the power under Article 226 of the Constitution of India is not on a par with the constitutional jurisdiction conferred upon this Court under Article 142 of the Constitution of India. The High Court has no jurisdiction to direct formulation of a new legal principle or a new procedure which would be contrary to and inconsistent with a statutory provision like the Code of Criminal Procedure. (See State of H.P. v. A Parent of a Student of Medical College and Asif Hameed v. State of J&K)."

In a Land Acquisition & Requisition matter, the Five Judge Bench of the Hon'ble Supreme Court in the case of **Gurpreet Singh Versus Union of India (2006) 8 SCC 457** has held that by way of clarification, the

Hon'ble Supreme Court can exercise its power under Article 141 and 142 of the Constitution with a view to avoiding the multiplicity of litigation on the matter not referred to it under Article 145 of the Constitution. The relevant paragraph 54 is reproduced as under:

"One other question also was sought to be raised and answered by this Bench though not referred to it. Considering that the question arises in various cases pending in courts all over the country, we permitted the counsel to address us on that question. That question is whether in the light of the decision in Sunder^2, the awardee/decree-holder would be entitled to claim interest on solatium in execution though it is not specifically granted by the decree. It is well settled that an execution court cannot go behind the decree. If, therefore, the claim for interest on solatium had been made and the same has been negatived either expressly or by necessary implication by the judgment or decree of the Reference Court or of the appellate court, the execution court will have necessarily to reject the claim for interest on solatium based on Sunder^2 on the ground that the execution court cannot go behind the decree. But if the award of the Reference Court or that of the appellate court does not specifically refer to the question of interest on solatium or in cases where claim had not been made and rejected either expressly or impliedly by the Reference Court or the appellate court, and merely interest on compensation is awarded, then it would be open to the execution court to apply the ratio of Sunder² and say that the compensation awarded includes solatium and in such an event interest on the amount could be directed to be deposited in execution. Otherwise, not. We also clarify that such interest on solatium can be claimed only in pending executions and not in closed executions and the execution court will be entitled to permit its recovery from the date of the judgment in Sunder² (19-9-2001) and not for any prior period. We also clarify that this will not entail any reappropriation or fresh appropriation by the decree-holder. This we have indicated by way of clarification also in exercise of our power under Articles 141 and 142 of the Constitution of India with a view to avoid multiplicity of litigation on this question."

In the case of **Secretary, State of Karnataka & Ors. Versus Umadevi & Ors., (2006) 4 SCC 1** the Constitution Bench of the Hon'ble Supreme Court by exercising the power under Article 142 of the Constitution has explained the significance of complete justice i.e. justice according to law and though it would be open to the Hon'ble Supreme Court to mould the relief and but it would not grant relief which would amount to perpetuating an illegality. Hence for dispensing complete justice under Article 142 of the Constitution, the Hon'ble Supreme Court would not normally give a go-by to the procedure established by law in the matter of public employment. In the said judgment it has been made clear that the wide powers under Article 226 are not intended to be used for the purpose of perpetuating irregularities, illegalities, or improprieties. In the said Uma Devi case, the Hon'ble Supreme Court has discussed the concept of "equal pay for equal work" in para 44. The Hon'ble Supreme Court has in its various decisions applied the principle of "equal pay for equal work" and has laid down the parameters for the application of that principle. However, the acceptance of that principle cannot lead to a position where the court could direct those appointments made without following the due procedure established by the law to be deemed to be permanent or issue directions to treat them permanently. It would not be just or proper to pass an order in the exercise of jurisdiction under Article 226 or 32 of the Constitution or in the exercise of power under Article 142 of the Constitution permitting those persons engaged to be observed or to be made permanent based on their appointments to be absorbed or to be made permanent based on their appointments or engagements. Complete justice would be justice according to law and it is open to the Supreme Court to mould the relief and would not grant a relief which would amount to perpetuating an illegality. In the said judgment, the Hon'ble Supreme Court has clarified that the decisions which run counter to the principle settled in this decision. At para 54, the Hon'ble Supreme Court has also clarified that those decisions which run counter to the principle settled, will stand denuded.

In this regard at para 55 of the said judgment reported in (2006) 4 SCC 1, the Hon'ble Supreme Court has elaborately discussed on various subjects and the power under Article 142 of the Constitution. The said paragraph 55 is reproduced herein below for the sake of general idea and knowledge of the citizens of our country:

"55. In cases relating to service in the Commercial Taxes Department, the High Court has directed that those engaged on daily wages, be paid wages equal to the salary and allowances that are being paid to the regular employees of their cadre in government service, with effect from the dates from which they were respectively appointed. The objection taken was to the direction for payment from the dates of engagement. We find that the High Court had clearly gone wrong in directing that these employees be paid salary equal to the salary and allowances that are being paid to the regular employees of their cadre in government service, with effect from the dates from which they were respectively engaged or appointed. It was not open to the High Court to impose such an obligation on the State when the very question before the High Court in the case was whether these employees were entitled to have equal pay for equal work so called and were entitled to any other benefit. They had also been engaged in the teeth of directions not to do so. We are, therefore, of the view that, at best, the Division Bench of the High Court should have directed that wages equal to the salary that is being paid to regular employees be paid to these daily-wage employees with effect from the date of its judgment. Hence, that part of the direction of the Division Bench is modified and it is directed that these daily-wage earners be paid wages equal to the salary at the lowest grade of employees of their cadre in the Commercial Taxes Department in government service, from the date of the judgment of the Division Bench of the High Court. Since, they are only daily-wage earners, there would be no question of other allowances being paid to them. In view of our conclusion, that the courts are not expected to issue directions for making such persons permanent in service, we set aside that part of the direction of the High Court directing the Government to consider their cases for regularization. We also notice that the High Court has not adverted to the aspect as to whether it was regularization or it was giving permanency that was being directed by the High Court. In such a situation, the direction in that regard will stand deleted and the appeals filed by the State would stand allowed to that extent. If sanctioned posts are vacant (they are said to be vacant) the State will take immediate steps for filling those posts by a regular process of selection. But when regular recruitment is undertaken, the respondents in CAs Nos.3595-612 and those in the Commercial Taxes Department similarly situated, will be allowed to compete, waiving the age restriction imposed for the recruitment and giving some weightage for their having been engaged for work in the Department for a significant period of time. That would be the extent of the exercise of power by this Court under Article 142 of the Constitution to do justice to them."

For complete justice, the Hon'ble Supreme Court by exercising the power under Article 142 of the Constitution in the case of **Manish Ratan & Ors. Versus State of M.P. & Anr., (2007) 1 SCC 262** transferred a criminal case from the court of the Chief Judicial Magistrate, Datia to the Court of the Chief Judicial Magistrate, Jabalpur in the matter of **Manish Ratan & Ors. Versus State of M.P. & Anr., (2007) 1 SCC 262** while transferring a criminal case in an appeal matter, the Hon'ble Supreme Court has given the reasons in the said judgment. The relevant paragraphs 16, 18 and 19 are reproduced as under:

"16. Yet again in Ramesh v. State of T.N., Abraham Ajith was followed by this Court stating: (SCC pp. 512-13, paras 11-12)

"11. In the view we are taking, it is not necessary for us to delve into the question of territorial jurisdiction of the Court at Trichy in detail. Suffice it to say that on looking at the complaint at its face value, the offences alleged cannot be said to have been committed wholly or partly within the local jurisdiction of the Magistrate's Court at Trichy. Prima facie, none of the ingredients constituting the offence can be said to have occurred within the local jurisdiction of that court. Almost all the allegations pertain to acts of cruelty for the purpose of extracting additional property as dowry while she was in the matrimonial home at Mumbai and the alleged acts of misappropriation of her movable property at Mumbai. However, there is one allegation relevant to Section 498-A from which it could be inferred that one of the acts giving rise to the offence under the said section had taken place in Chennai. It is alleged that when the relations of the informant met her in-laws at a hotel in Chennai where they were staying on 13-10-1998, there was again a demand for dowry and a threat to torture her in case she was sent back to Mumbai without the money and articles demanded.

12. Thus the alleged acts which according to the petitioner constitute the offences under Sections 498-A and 406 were done by the accused mostly in Mumbai and partly in Chennai. Prima facie, there is nothing in the entire complaint which goes to show that any acts constituting the alleged offences were at all committed at Trichy."

18. We, therefore, are of the opinion that, interest of justice would be subserved, while setting aside the order of the High Court, if in exercise of our jurisdiction under Article 142 of the Constitution of India, we direct transfer of the criminal case pending in the Court of Chief Judicial Magistrate, Datia to the

Court of Chief Judicial Magistrate, Jabalpur. We accordingly do so.

19. Although the complainant has filed an application before us for impleading herself as a party, nobody has appeared on her behalf. We, therefore, direct the Chief Judicial Magistrate, Jabalpur to issue notice to her. Keeping in view of the fact that Respondent 2 is residing at Datia, we would request the Chief Judicial Magistrate, Jabalpur to issue notice to her. Keeping in view of the fact that Respondent 2 is residing at Datia, we would request the Chief Judicial Magistrate, Jabalpur to accommodate her in the matter of fixing the date(s) of hearing as far as possible."

In the case of **Central Bank of India & Ors. Versus Madan Chandra Brahma & Anr., (2007) 8 SCC 294,** the Hon'ble Supreme Court has exercised the power under Article 142 of the Constitution. Para 16 and 17 of the said judgment are relevant which contemplate as under:

"16. Having held on law that the respondent is not entitled to the relief claimed by him, we feel that some compensation should be directed to be paid to him, in the circumstances, in exercise of our jurisdiction under Article 142 of the Constitution of India. The respondent, we notice, was fighting on a question of interpretation of the Regulation of the appellant Bank and has remained in Court for a considerable time. Taking note of the divergence in the views of the High

Court, our conclusion and the circumstances of the case, we feel that it would be appropriate to direct the appellant to pay a sum of Rs.1 lakh to the respondent ex gratia. We clarify that the direction is not intended to be a precedent in any manner.

17. We, therefore, allow this appeal and setting aside the decision of the High Court dismiss the writ petition filed by Respondent 1 in the High Court. We direct the appellant to pay a sum of Rs.1 lakh to Respondent 1 ex gratia within three months from today. In the circumstances, we direct the parties to suffer their costs here and in the High Court."

In the matter of **Jacob Mathew Versus State of Punjab & Anr., (2005) 6 SCC 1**, the Hon'ble Supreme Court was pleased to reverse the order of the High Court by exercising the plenary power under Articles 142 and 141 of the Constitution and prescribed the guidelines for prosecuting the medical professionals for criminal negligence. The relevant paragraphs 50 and 51 of the said judgment are reproduced as under:

"50. As we have noticed hereinabove that the cases of doctors (surgeons and physicians) being subjected to criminal prosecution are on an increase. Sometimes such prosecutions are filed by private complainants and sometimes by the police on an FIR being lodged and cognizance taken. The investigating officer and the private complainant cannot always be supposed to have knowledge of medical science so as to determine whether the act of the accused medical professional amounts to a rash or negligent act within the domain of criminal law under Section 304-A IPC. The criminal process once initiated subjects the medical professional to serious embarrassment and sometimes harassment. He has to seek bail to escape arrest, which may or may not be granted to him. At the end he may be exonerated by acquittal or discharge but the loss which he has suffered to his reputation cannot be compensated by any standards."

"51. We may not be understood as holding that doctors can never be prosecuted for an offence of which rashness or negligence is an essential ingredient. All that we are doing is to emphasize the need for care and caution in the interest of society; for, the service which the medical profession renders to human beings is probably the noblest of all, and hence there is a need for protecting doctors from frivolous or unjust prosecutions. Many a complainant prefer recourse to criminal process as a tool for pressurizing the medical professional for extracting uncalled for or unjust compensation. Such malicious proceedings have to be guarded against."

In the case of **Mohd. Shamim & Ors. Versus Smt. Nahid Begum & Anr., (2005) 3 SCC 302**, the Hon'ble Supreme Court considering the facts of the case substantially based on the settlement arrived at between the parties was pleased to set aside the High

Court judgment and also quash the FIR registered under Section 406/498-A/34 of the IPC by exercising the jurisdiction under Article 142 of the Constitution. The relevant paragraph 16 of the said judgment is reproduced as under:

"16. In view of the conduct of the first respondent in entering into the aforementioned settlement, the continuance of the criminal proceeding pending against the appellants, in our opinion, in this case also, would be an abuse of the process of the court. Appellant 1, however, would be entitled to withdraw the sum of Rs.50,000 which has been deposited in the court. We, therefore, in exercise of our jurisdiction under Article 142 of the Constitution direct that the impugned judgment be aside. The first information report lodged against the appellants is quashed. The appeal is allowed. However, this order should not be treated as a precedent."

The Supreme Court can also order for suo-motu enquiry by exercising the power under Article 142 of the Constitution as it has happened in a case where the Hon'ble Supreme Court was pleased to issue suo-motu notice after going through the news item "**Madhepura in a Tizzy Over Pappu Visit" in The Times of India dated 05.05.2004**. For the sake of complete justice, the Hon'ble Supreme Court had no other option but to take suo-motu action in the interest of the public. The said order was reported in **(2004) 5 SCC 124** and the relevant part of the same is reproduced as under:-

"2. Notice be issued to the Home Secretary, State of Bihar who will also inform this Court, how many days during his custody period he has spent in the hospital, if so, what were facilities provided to him in the hospital. The Jail Superintendent concerned will also file an affidavit explaining the circumstances under which he was permitted to go out of the jail.

3. This direction of ours to the State of Bihar will not be a bar for any action or investigation/inquiry that may be conducted by the Election Commission and decision taken thereon. The Home Secretary, State of Bihar and Jail Superintendent concerned will file an affidavit within eight weeks from today."

In a case i.e. **Harigovind Yadav Versus Rewa Sidhi Gramin Bank & Ors. (2006) 6 SCC 145**, the Hon'ble Supreme Court in a promotional matter was pleased to issue direction for the sake of complete justice to the Petitioner by exercising the power under Article 142 of the Constitution to promote the Petitioner as a field supervisor by the Respondent Bank. However, it was made clear in the order that the Petitioner would be entitled to monetary benefits flowing from such promotion only prospectively, though the pay was to be refixed with reference to the retrospective date of promotion. While issuing direction to the Respondent bank as stated hereinabove, the Hon'ble Supreme Court was pleased to hold as under:

"21. It is thus clear that this Court did not accept the promotion policy contained in the circular dated 2-2-1989 as being in consonance with the principle of seniority-cum-merit. This Court held that the policy which did not prescribe a minimum standard for assessing merit and which promoted candidates on the basis of comparative merit, with reference to total marks obtained by the eligible candidates, followed the merit-cum-seniority principle. The decision in Sivaiah[1] relating to Area/ Senior Managers of the first respondent Bank was followed by the High Court in the case of the appellant, in its judgment dated 13-10-1998 and it was held that the procedure adopted by the first respondent Bank for promotion of the third respondent and V.P. Singh as per the circular dated 2-2-1989 was contrary to the Rules which required promotions by seniority-cum-merit, and the Bank was directed to redo the promotions by considering the case of the appellant and other eligible candidates by adopting the criteria of seniority-cum-merit. The decision attained finality as the appeal and SLP were rejected. It may be stated that even prior to the decision in Sivaiah[1] relating to Area/Senior Managers of the first respondent Bank, the same view had been expressed in the earlier judgment dated 9-10-1996 of the Division Bench of the Madhya Pradesh High Court in LPA No.151 of 1996 and connected cases and civil appeals arising out of SLPs (C) Nos.17780-81 of 1997 filed against the said judgment dated 9-10-1996 had been dismissed. Therefore, we have several rounds of litigation which had been fought up to this Court where the High Court and this Court have repeatedly and clearly held that the procedure prescribed, in the promotion policy circular dated 2-2-1989, is not in consonance with the principle of seniority-cum-merit prescribed for promotion under the Rules but amounted to following the principle of merit-cum-seniority and therefore vitiated. What is surprising is that, in spite of these decisions, the first respondent Bank again adopted the very same procedure contained in the promotion policy of 2-2-1989 and again failed to promote the appellant by assigning him marks of 16(20), 10(10), 3(5), 24(40) and 9(25) and held that he was not eligible for promotion as he did not secure the minimum marks of 10 prescribed for interview. But, admittedly, there was no overall minimum and the procedure required assessment of comparative merit. This is not therefore a case of the appellant failing to secure the minimum necessary merit required for promotion but a case where the appellant's entitlement to promotion was sought to be assessed by adopting a procedure which allotted 20 marks for seniority, 40 marks for performance, 15 marks for posting at rural and difficult centres and 25 marks for interview. The Bank has persisted in adopting the merit-cum-seniority procedure in spite of the decisions of this Court in several rounds of litigation referred to above. As the entire promotion procedure adopted by the Bank as per its policy dated 2-2-1989 has stood rejected by the High Court and this

Court in Sivaiah[1] as also in the earlier round of litigation of the appellant, the promotion of the third respondent and non-promotion of the appellant by adopting the very same procedure is liable to be interfered with."

The framers of the Constitution have also intuitively thrust upon the Hon'ble Supreme Court in an anomalous case under Article 142 of the Constitution to expunge the unnecessary adverse remarks against any person. In the matter of **"K" Judicial Officer reported in (2001) 3 SCC 54** wherein the Hon'ble Supreme Court in a Criminal Appeal matter by exercising the power under Article 136 and /or Article 142 of the Constitution of India was pleased to expunge the adverse remarks not necessary for the decision of the case. Therefore, the Hon'ble Supreme Court expunged the remarks of the Hon'ble High Court. The relevant paragraph 19 of the said judgment is reproduced as under:

"Reverting back to the case at hand, may be that the learned Metropolitan Magistrate in initiating contempt proceedings and taking cognizance of substantive offences under the Indian Penal Code against the officials of Public Works Department was not properly advised or was at the worst indulging in a misadventure and therefore to the extent of quashing of the proceedings by the High Court we may not find fault and certainly no one has come up to this Court complaining against the merits of that part of the order of the High Court by which criminal proceedings have been quashed. Nevertheless, the ill-advised move or misadventure of the learned Metropolitan Magistrate was neither a misconduct nor an outcome of malice. Though she acted in a way which did not meet the approval of the High Court, the facts and the circumstances of the case point out that her only desire was to make her courtroom functional. Probably she felt aggrieved, rather agitated, by the apathy of the Public Works Department people who were taking things too easy, unmindful of the practical difficulties faced by the Presiding Judge occupying the courtroom and discharging judicial functions. The fact remains that the observations were made by the High Court without affording the Metropolitan Magistrate an opportunity of explaining or defending herself. The remarks were not necessary for the decision of the case by the High Court as an integral part thereof. Animadverting on the conduct of the learned Metropolitan Magistrate was not a necessity for the exercise by the High Court of inherent power or the power of superintendence to quash the proceedings initiated by the learned Metropolitan Magistrate. Expunging of the remarks, as we propose to do, will not affect the reasons for the judgment of the High Court. On the other hand, the remarks have a potential to prejudice the career of the appellant."

The Hon'ble Supreme Court can transfer the prisoners, under-trials, detenues or convicts from one prison to another by exercising the powers under Article 142 of the Constitution for the sake of complete justice. In the case of **Kalyan Chandra Sarkar Versus Rajesh Ranjan @ Pappu Yadav & Anr. (2005) 3 SCC 284** since there was no provision under Section 3 of the Transfer of Prisoners Act, 1950 the Hon'ble Supreme Court was pleased to order the transfer of the Respondent from Beur Jail, Patna to Tihar Jail, Delhi. The relevant paragraph 47 of the said judgment is reproduced as under:

"In compliance with this order, we direct the State of Bihar to transfer the respondent from Beur Jail, Patna to Tihar Jail, Delhi and hand over the prisoner to the authorized officer by prior intimation to Tihar Jail authorities of his arrival in Delhi. The authorities escorting the respondent from Patna to Delhi shall strictly follow the rules applicable to the transit prisoners and no special privilege should be shown; any such act if proved, will be taken serious note of. The respondent shall be transferred to Tihar Jail from Patna within one week from the date of this order. A copy of this order shall forthwith be communicated to the Home Secretary, Government of Bihar, Superintendent of Beur Adarsh Jail and the Inspector General, Prisons, Tihar Jail. We further direct that all authorities, civil and judicial, shall act in aid of this order of this Court as contemplated under Article 144 of the Constitution."

The words "complete justice" mentioned in the Article 142(1) are meant to supplement the existing legal provision for the Hon'ble Supreme Court to dispense the complete justice between the parties and not to supplant. It is conceived to meet the situation where it is a hard nut to crack and to find an effective and appropriate solution. The analogous provision relating to complete justice is available under **Article 104 of the Constitution of Bangladesh**. The same is reproduced as under:

"104. The Appellate Division shall have power to issue such directions, orders, decrees or writs as may be necessary for doing complete justice in any cause or matter pending before it, including orders for the purpose of securing the attendance of any person or the discovery or production of any document."

The provision under Article 142 of the Constitution of India is like a panpharmacon endowed with the Hon'ble Supreme Court of India by the Constitution of India to do complete justice. The magnanimity and the amplitude of Article 142 of the Constitution of India help the Hon'ble Supreme Court dispense complete justice. The framers of the Constitution while drafting the provision under Article 142 of the Constitution have plunged deep into the future perspective of the myriad problems of the citizens. Therefore, we should owe the framers of our Constitution and express deep gratitude to them for taking care of the citizens governed by the Constitution.

The Hon'ble Supreme Court by exercising the power under Article 142 of the Constitution has been pleased to grant divorce and thereby has also passed the decree of dissolution of marriage pending before the trial court. In the case of **Reshmi Shaw alias Gupta Versus Bidesh Kumar Gupta reported in (2024) SCC OnLine SC 556**, the Hon'ble Supreme Court was pleased to dissolve the marriage between the parties by exercising the power under Article 142 of the Constitution in a matrimonial dispute filed before the Family Court under Section 13 of the Hindu Marriage Act, 1955. The relevant paragraph 3 of the said judgment is reproduced as under:

"After having perused the Settlement Agreement, we are of the view that this is a fit case for this Court to exercise its power under Article 142 of the Constitution of India to dissolve the marriage between the parties. Hence, we pass the following order:

(1) The cases pending between the parties as mentioned in paragraphs 6 & 7 shall be withdrawn by them.

(2) The amount of Rs.12 lakhs towards full and final settlement as detailed in paragraph 5-A of the settlement agreement shall be paid to the petitioner-wife by the respondent-husband.

(3) The marriage solemnized between the parties on 03.05.2021 is hereby dissolved by a decree of divorce

under Section 13-B of the Hindu Marriage Act, 1955; and

(4) The parties shall diligently abide by the terms of the Settlement Agreement.

(5) The decree of divorce shall be drawn incorporating all the terms and conditions of the Settlement Agreement within a period of six weeks from today."

The Hon'ble Supreme Court in the case of **Bharat Sewa Sansthan Versus U.P. Electronics Corporation Limited (2007) 7 SCC 737** for doing complete justice has held that the nature and ambit of power under Article 142 of the Constitution of India no doubt is meant to do complete justice between the mitigating parties but at the same time the Supreme Court has to bear in mind that the power is conceived to meet the situations which cannot be effectively and appropriately tackled by existing provisions of law. The relevant parts of paragraphs 25 and 26 are reproduced as under: -

"25. Now, the question pressed before us is whether we should, in exercise of our power and jurisdiction under Article 142 of the Constitution of India as submitted by Shri Shanti Bhushan, grant the payment of balance of arrears of rent, payment of balance arrears of water and sewerage tax and interest on the arrears of rent to the appellant Sansthan, which amounts are disputed by the respondent corporation before us. The nature and ambit of the power of this

Court under Article 142 of the Constitution of India, no doubt, is meant to do complete justice between the litigating parties, but at the same time this Court has to bear in mind that the power is conceived to meet the situations which cannot be effectively and appropriately tackled by the existing provisions of law."

"26. Human and equitable approach should be balanced to do complete justice to both the parties and not be tilted in favour of either party ignoring the statutory provisions. This Court in exercise of its jurisdiction can grant appropriate relief where there is some manifest illegality, or where there is manifest want of jurisdiction, or where some palpable injustice is shown to have resulted to the parties."

Even the Single Judge of the Hon'ble Supreme Court for doing complete justice can exercise the power under Article 142 of the Constitution. In this regard the relevant paragraph 41 of the judgment in the case of **Rhea Chakraborty Versus The State of Bihar T.P.(Crl.) No.225 of 2020; [AIR 2020 SC 3826]** is reproduced as under:

"41. In such backdrop, to ensure public confidence in the investigation and to do complete justice in the matter, this Court considers it appropriate to invoke the powers conferred by Article 142 of the Constitution. As a Court exercising lawful jurisdiction for the assigned roster, no impediment is seen for exercise of plenary power in the present matter. Therefore while according approval for the ongoing CBI investigation, if any other case is registered on the death of the actor Sushant Singh Rajput and the surrounding circumstances of his unnatural death, the CBI is directed to investigate the new case as well. It is ordered accordingly."

The Hon'ble Single Judge of the Hon'ble Supreme Court can exercise the power under Article 142 of the Constitution to dissolve the marriage between the parties as decided in the matter of **Sabita Shashank Singh Versus Shashank Shekhar Singh in T.P. (Civil) No. 908 of 2019**. The relevant paragraphs 4 and 9 of the judgment are reproduced as under:

"4. As per settlement arrived at between the parties, a demand draft amounting to Rs.90,00,000/- (Rupees Ninety Lakhs Only) has been made over to the petitioner in our presence, which she has accepted unconditionally upon disposal of the proceedings in terms of the settlement agreement executed between the parties and their advocates on 15.02.2021."

"9. Resultantly, application No.30625/2021 is allowed and the Transfer Petition is disposed of in the aforementioned terms."

In a case Hon'ble Supreme Court in Prem Chand Garg Vs. Excise Commissioner, U.P. Allahabad (1963) Supp. (1) SCR 885 wherein under Article 32 an interesting and important question about the validity of one of the rules made by the Hon'ble Supreme Court in exercising its powers under Article 145 of the Constitution was challenged. The impugned rule was Rule 12 of Order XXXVII which provided that the court might in the proceedings (to which the said order applied) and impose such terms as to costs and as to giving of security as the Hon'ble Supreme Court thought fit at that time. The Petitioners Prem Chand Garg, 8 Anr., partners of M/s Industrial Chemical Corporation, Ghaziabad filed a Writ Petition under Article 32 bearing no. W.P.(Civil) No.348 of 1961 impeaching the validity of the order passed by the Excise Commissioner refusing permission to the distillery to supply power alcohol to the Petitioner. The said petition was admitted on 12th December, 1961 and a rule was ordered to be issued to the Respondents. The Excise Commissioner of U.P. Allahabad and the State of U.P. at the time when the rule was issued, the Hon'ble Supreme Court directed the Petitioner to deposit a security of Rs.2,500/- in cash within six weeks. According to the practice of the Hon'ble Supreme Court prevailing at that time this order was treated as a condition precedent for issuing a rule nisi to the impleaded Respondents. The Petitioner found it difficult to raise this amount and showed it on January 24, 1962. They moved the Supreme Court for modification of that order as a security. That application was dismissed but further time was given to deposit the said amount by March 26, 1962. In the said petition, the Petitioners contended that the impugned rule giving of security is ultra-vires because it contravened the fundamental rights guaranteed to the Petitioner under Article 32 of the Constitution. But the Hon'ble Supreme Court was pleased to hold as under:-

"Held, (per Sinha, C.J., Gajendragadkar, Wanchoo and Das Gupta, JJ., Shah, J., contra), that r.12 of O.XXXV Supreme Court Rules is invalid in so far as it relates to the furnishing of security. The right to move the Supreme Court under Art.32 is an absolute right and the content of this right cannot be circumscribed or impaired on any ground. An order for furnishing security for the respondent's costs retards the assertion or vindication of the fundamental right under Art.32 and contravenes the said right. The fact that the rule is discretionary does not alter the position. Though Art.142(1) empowers the Supreme Court to pass any order to do complete justice between the parties, the Court cannot make an order inconsistent with the fundamental rights guaranteed by Part III of the Constitution. No question of inconsistency between Art.142(1) and Art.32 arises as Art.142(1) does not confer any power on the Supreme Court to contravene the provisions of Art.32. Nor does Art.145 which confers power upon the Supreme Court to make rules, empower it to contravene the provisions of Art.32.

Ramesh Thapper v. State of Madras, [1950] S.C.R. 594, State of Madras v. V.G. Row, [1952] S.C.R. 597 and Daryao v. State of U.P., [1962] 1 S.C.R. 574, relied on.

Kavalappara Kottarathil Kochunni Moopil Nayar v. State of Madras, [1959] Supp. 2 S.C.R. 316, explained.

Pandit M.S.M. Sharma v. Shri Sri Krishna Sinha, [159] Supp. 1 S.C.R. 806, K.M. Nanavati v. State of Bombay, [1961] 1 S.C.R. 497, distinguished.

Shah, J. – The impugned rule is not void. The rule does not directly place any restriction upon the right of a litigant to move the Supreme Court. It merely recognizes the jurisdiction of the Court, in appropriate cases, to make an order demanding security. It is not, in substance, a rule relating to practice and procedure but it deals primarily with the jurisdiction of the Court, which has its source in Art. 142 of the Constitution. No question of conflict arises between the rule which merely declares the jurisdiction of the Court defined by Art. 142 and the right guaranteed under Art.32. The provisions of Art.142 and Art.32(1) must be read harmoniously. Both being provisions in the Constitution, one cannot prevail over the other.

Pandit M.S.M. Sharma v. Shri Sri Krishna Sinha, [1959] Supp. 1 S.C.R. 806, relied on.

ORIGINAL JURISDICTION : Petition No.52 of 1962.

Petition under Art.32 of the Constitution of India for enforcement of fundamental rights.

G.S. Pathak, R. Gopalakrishnan and Naunit Lal, for the petitioners.

K.S. Hajela and C.P. Lal, for the respondents Nos.1 & 2.

C.K. Daphtary, Solicitor-General of India, B.R.L. Iyengar and R.H. Dhebar, for respondent No.3.

1962. November, 6. The Judgment of Sinha, C.J., Gajendragadkar, Wanchoo and Das Gupta, JJ., was delivered by Gajendragadkar, J. Shah J., delivered a separate Judgment."

The Hon'ble Supreme Court has also elaborately discussed in the said judgment the power under Article 142 and/or the Article 32 and held as under:

"The impugned rule being merely declaratory of the jurisdiction which is defined by Art.142 of the Constitution no question of conflict between law made by the State, and the guarantee of right to move this Court under Art.32(1) by appropriate proceedings for enforcement of fundamental rights arises. The provisions of the Constitution contained in Art.142 and Art.32(1) must be read harmoniously. On the one hand there is the guaranteed right in favour of the litigant by an appropriate proceeding to move this Court for enforcement of a fundamental right, on the other there is the jurisdiction vested in this Court to pass all such orders as may be necessary in the interests of justice – such orders including inappropriate cases an order for payment of costs by the petitioner. There is no warrant for assuming that the exercise of this jurisdiction has to be subordinated to the exercise of the right to move this Court. Article 32(1) is included in Ch.III and the right to move this Court is itself made a fundamental right, whereas Art.142 falls in Part V dealing with Union Judiciary. But these being parts of a Constitutional document no special sanctity attaches to the provisions contained in Ch.III so as to prevail over the other provisions. In *Pandit M.S.M. Sharma v. Shri Sri Krishna Sinha*([1]), this Court had to consider whether Art.194 dealing with the powers, privileges and immunities of the State Legislatures and of their members was subordinate to fundamental right of speech under Art.19(1)(a) of the Constitution. The petitioner in that case urged that rights, powers and privileges of the members of the House of Commons in England which could be claimed by the members of the State Legislatures by virtue of Art.194 had still to stand the test of reasonableness prescribed by Art.19(2), and to the extent of inconsistency the right had to yield before the fundamental right guaranteed by Art.19(1). It was held by the Court that Art.19(1)(a) and Art.194 have to be harmoniously interpreted and the only method of reconciling the two is to read the general provision of Art.19(1)(a) as subject to Art.194 just as Art.31 is read as subject to Art.265. Generality of the provision is not however the sole criterion. Clause (1) and (2) of Art.13 render laws either pre-existing or enacted since the Constitution, void if they are inconsistent with or take away or abridge any fundamental rights. Exercise of legislative authority under powers derived from the

Constitution is undoubtedly hit by Art.13(2). But one part of the Constitution cannot render nugatory another part: the two must be read together and harmonized. So read, the guarantee of the right to move this Court by appropriate proceedings, for enforcement of fundamental rights cannot be permitted to encroach upon the jurisdiction of the Court, where exercise thereof is necessary for doing complete justice. Therefore even in a proceeding under Art.32(1), this Court is competent to make all such orders as it deems proper including an order for security for costs of the respondent.

The impugned rule which enunciates the jurisdiction of the Court to impose terms as to giving of security is not therefore void.

BY COURT: In accordance with the opinion of the majority of the writ petition is allowed and the order calling upon the petitioners to furnish security of Rs.2,500/- is set aside. There will be no order as to costs."

Later on, in the case of a seven judge bench titled A.R. Antulay Versus R.S. Nayak & Anr. reported in (1988) 2 SCC 602, the Hon'ble Supreme Court has also referred the case of Prem Chand Garg Versus State of U.P. and cited the said case at para 50, 100 and 178 for clarifying the power of the Hon'ble Supreme Court under Article 142 (1), Article 32 as well as Article 145 of the Constitution. The relevant parts of the said paragraphs are reproduced herein below:

"50. This Court by majority held that Rule 12 of Order XXXV of the Supreme Court Rules was invalid insofar as it related to the furnishing of security. The right to move the Supreme Court, it was emphasized, under Article 32 was an absolute right and the content of this right could not be circumscribed or impaired on any ground and an order for furnishing security for the respondent's costs retarded and contravened the said right. The fact that the rule was discretionary did not alter the position. Though Article 142(1) empowers the Supreme Court to pass any order to do complete justice between the parties, the court cannot make an order inconsistent with the fundamental rights guaranteed by Part III of the Constitution. No question of inconsistency between Article 142 (1) and Article 32 arose. Gajendragadkar, J. speaking for the majority of the judges of this Court said that Article 142(1) did not confer any power on this Court to contravene the provisions of Article 32 of the Constitution."

"100. ......"It would thus be seen that the main controversy in the case of *Prem Chand Garg* centred round the question as to whether Article 145 conferred powers on this Court to make rules, though they may be inconsistent with the constitutional provisions prescribed by Part III. Once it was held that the powers under Article 142 had to be read subject not only to the fundamental rights, but to other binding statutory provisions, it became clear that the rule which authorized the making of the impugned order was invalid. It was in that context that the validity of the order had to be incidentally examined. The petition was made not to challenge the order as such, but to challenge the validity of the rule under which the order was made. Once the rule was struck down as being invalid, the order passed under the said rule had to be vacated. It is difficult to see how this decision can be pressed into service by Mr. Setalvad in support of the argument that a judicial order passed by this Court was held to be subject to the writ jurisdiction of this Court itself.

In view of this decision in *Mirajkar case* it must be taken as concluded that judicial proceedings in this Court are not subject to the writ jurisdiction thereof."

"178. Learned Chief Justice referring to the scope of the matter that fell for consideration in *Garg case* stated : (SCR p. 766)

It would thus be seen that the main controversy in the case of *Prem Chand Garg* centered round the question as to whether Article 145 conferred powers on this Court to make rules, though they may be inconsistent with the constitutional provisions prescribed by Part III. Once it was held that the powers under Article 142 had to be read subject not only to the fundamental rights, but to other binding statutory provisions, it became clear that the rule which authorized the making of the impugned order was invalid. It was in that context that the validity of the order had to be incidentally examined. The petition was made not to challenge the order as such, but to challenge the validity of the rule under which the order was made."

In a batch of Transfer Petitions (Civil and Criminal) involving the matrimonial dispute under Section 13-B of the Hindu Marriage Act, 1955, in the matter of Shilpa Shailesh Versus Varun Sreenivasan reported in (2023) SCC OnLine SC 544, the constitution bench of the Hon'ble Supreme Court was pleased to decide an issue i.e. "whether the period prescribed in sub-section (2) of Section 13-B of the Hindu Marriage Act, 1955 can be waived or reduced by this court in the exercise of its jurisdiction under Article 142 of the Constitution?". It is pertinent to mention sub-section (2) of Section 13-B of the Hindu Marriage Act, 1955 as under:

"[13B. Divorce by mutual consent.- (1) ...

(2) On the motion of both the parties made not earlier than six months after the date of the presentation of the petition referred to in sub-section (1) and not later than eighteen months after the said date, if the petition is not withdrawn in the meantime, the court shall, on being satisfied, after hearing the parties and after making such inquiry as it thinks fit, that a marriage has been solemnized and that the averments in the petition are true, pass a decree of divorce declaring the

marriage to be dissolved with effect from the date of the decree.]"

The Constitution Bench of the Hon'ble Supreme Court while deciding a particular issue in a Transfer Petition, was pleased to hear the Attorney General for India who suggested two additional questions of law in his written submissions as it is apparent from paragraphs 4 and 5 of the above mentioned judgment Shilpa Shailesh Versus Varun Sreenivasan reported in (2023) SCC OnLine SC 544 reproduced as under:

"4. The Attorney General for India, in Para 5 of his written submissions, had suggested two additional questions of law, which read thus:

"In view of the decisions of the Hon'ble Court in the above cases, the view of the Hon'ble Court that divorce can be granted on the ground of "irretrievable breakdown of marriage" even in the absence of such ground being contemplated by the legislature may require consideration by the Constitution Bench.

Similarly, the issue as to whether the period prescribed in sub-section (2) of Section 13-B of the Hindu Marriage Act, 1955 can be waived or reduced by this Court in exercise of its jurisdiction under Article 142 of the Constitution also requires consideration by the Constitution Bench."

"5. T.P.(C) No. 1118 of 2014 was effectively disposed of vide the order dated 06.05.2015 dissolving the marriage by grant of divorce by mutual consent with the two judges' bench exercising jurisdiction under Article 142 of the Constitution of India. However, in view the conflicting ratio of the judgments of this Court under Article 142 of the Constitution of India, the two judge' bench of this Court deferred the transfer petition to remain pending for statistical purposes, and formulated the following questions of law to be decided by a three judges' bench: (*Shilpa Sailesh case,* SCC pp. 353-354, paras 4-5)

"4. Notwithstanding the above order passed by us, for the purposes of statistics the present transfer petitions shall remain pending as we are of the view that an issue of some importance needs to be addressed by the Court in view of the huge number of requests for exercise of power under Article 142 of the Constitution that has confronted this Court consequent to settlement arrived at by and between the husband and the wife to seek divorce by mutual consent.

5. The questions are formulated herein below:

5.1. What could be the broad parameters for exercise of powers under Article 142 of the Constitution to dissolve a marriage between the consenting parties without referring the parties to the Family Court to wait for the mandatory period prescribed under Section 13-B of the Hindu Marriage Act.

5.2. Whether the exercise of such jurisdiction under Article 142 should not be made at all or whether such exercise should be left to be determined in the facts of every case."

After hearing the counsels for the parties including the Learned Attorney General for India, the Hon'ble Supreme Court by exercising the plenary power under Article 142 of the Constitution was pleased to dispose of all the Transfer Petitions civil and criminal. At the same time the Hon'ble Supreme Court in conclusion answered affirmative all the three questions framed in paragraphs 73, 74, 75 and 76 reproduced as under:

"73. In view of the aforesaid discussion, we decide this reference by answering the questions framed in the following manner:

(i) The scope and ambit of power and jurisdiction of this Court under Article 142(1) of the Constitution of India.

74. This question as to the power and jurisdiction of this Court under Article 142(1) of the Constitution of India is answered in terms of paragraphs 9 to 21, inter alia, holding that this Court can depart from the procedure as well as the substantive laws, as long as the decision is exercised based on considerations of fundamental general and specific public policy. While deciding whether to exercise discretion, this Court must consider the substantive provisions as enacted and not ignore the same, albeit this Court acts as a problem solver by balancing out equities between the

conflicting claims. This power is to be exercised in a 'cause or matter'.

(ii) In view of, and depending upon the findings of this bench on the first question, whether this Court, while hearing a transfer petition, or in any other proceedings, can exercise power under Article 142(1) of the Constitution, in view of the settlement between the parties, and grant a decree of divorce by mutual consent dispensing with the period and the procedure prescribed under Section 13-B of the Hindu Marriage Act, and also quash and dispose of other/connected proceedings under the Domestic Violence Act, Section 125 of the Cr.P.C., or criminal prosecution primarily under Section 498-A and other provisions of the I.P.C. If the answer to this question is in the affirmative, in which cases and under what circumstances should this Court exercise jurisdiction under Article 142 of the Constitution of India is an ancillary issue to be decided.

75. In view of our findings on the first question, this question has to be answered in the affirmative, *inter alia*, holding that this Court, in view of settlement between the parties, has the discretion to dissolve the marriage by passing a decree of divorce by mutual consent, without being bound by the procedural requirement to move the second motion. This power should be exercised with care and caution, keeping in mind the factors stated in *Amardeep Singh* (supra) and

Amit Kumar (supra). This Court can also, in exercise of power under Article 142(1) of the Constitution of India, quash and set aside other proceedings and orders, including criminal proceedings.

(iii) Whether this Court can grant divorce in exercise of power under Article 142(1) of the Constitution of India when there is complete and irretrievable breakdown of marriage in spite of the other spouses opposing the prayer?

76. This question is also answered in the affirmative, *inter alia*, holding that this Court, in exercise of power under Article 142(1) of the Constitution of India, has the discretion to dissolve the marriage on the ground of its irretrievable breakdown. This discretionary power is to be exercised to do 'complete justice' to the parties, wherein this Court is satisfied that the facts established show that the marriage has completely failed and there is no possibility that the parties will cohabit together, and continuation of the formal legal relationship is unjustified. The Court, as a court of equity, is required to also balance the circumstances and the background in which the party opposing the dissolution is placed."

Therefore, the framers of the Constitution by applying their intuitive power have incorporated the most powerful and pragmatic provision under Article 142 of the Constitution vesting with the Hon'ble Supreme Court to exercise the plenary power to pass such decree or make such order as is necessary for doing complete justice in any cause or matter pending before it.

THE SCOPE OF THE ARTICLE 142 OF THE CONSTITUTION OF INDIA:

The Article 142 vests the Supreme Court with the discretionary power in appropriate circumstances to deliver complete justice. In a given case where it is found the laws are inadequate for the purpose of granting relief, the Hon'ble Supreme Court can exercise its jurisdiction under Article 142 of the Constitution to do complete justice. The directions or the orders issued by the Hon'ble Supreme Court under Article 142 of the Constitution form the law of the land in the absence of any substantive law. Therefore, the power vested with the Hon'ble Supreme Court under Article 142 of the Constitution is just like a panpharmacon to redress the grievances of the parties in a case before the Hon'ble Court until the legislature enacts an appropriate and substantive law. By exercising the power under Article 142, the Hon'ble Supreme Court can grant relief to a party even who is not before the Hon'ble Court. Hence the paramount object of Article 142 is to ensure justice to the parties deserving it and thereby to prevent injustice to them.

OVERVIEW:

Article 142 (1) of the Constitution of India grants the Hon'ble Supreme Court, the power to pass such decrees or orders to do complete justice in any matter or cause pending before it for adjudication. The decrees and the orders are enforceable throughout India in the manner prescribed by the Parliament.

www.ingramcontent.com/pod-product-compliance
Lightning Source LLC
LaVergne TN
LVHW061558070526
838199LV00077B/7092